PROSI

MORE THAN AN ATTITUDE

A

PRACTICAL USE OF THE LAW

by

Alyce Bartholomew Soden

This book is dedicated to my beloved husband, Cecil James Soden, Jr., who has given me inspiration, support, and encouragement in my ministry and the writing of these pages, as well as being my practitioner-in-residence and confidant.

To my mentor Rev. Marion Parrish Hall and to Rev. John Hall whose tireless effort in editing are greatly appreciated.

The cartoons are courtesy of Mindy Eisman.

Graphics and designs are by Jim Soden.

Introduction

Our Universe operates on physical and spiritual laws; just as there is a law of gravity, there is a law of cause and effect.

You will discover or rediscover that the Universe acts upon your thought according to law.

As you read and discover the truth within, please remember the stories and analogies really happened and are true. The discoveries revealed are a lifetime of trial and error and experimenting. The author makes no claim to inventing or discovering spiritual laws. The purpose of this book is to reveal the power each of us wields and provide tools to use them effectively.

Much controversy exists regarding their existence, but as you learn to use these principles, you make the discoveries for yourself, which is the only way to achieve true prosperity.

TABLE OF CONTENTS

Chapter 1

FAITH BUILDING

What is your belief about money: root of all evil, hard to come by, easy go, never enough no matter how I stretch it, have to keep my nose to the grindstone to get ahead, poverty is next to Godliness?

Does your attitude about money bear out your experience?It usually does. That is the Principle. " It is done unto you as you believe."/1 And from the belief in lack, you reenact it in your life.

Do you hear yourself saying," If I'm careful, this will last until my next pay check," or "I can't afford that," or "Prices are so high,I don't want too much, just enough to get by." "I'm on a fixed income, you know!" etc.

Are you on a fixed income ? Most people are. You get so much, until you have been with the company a year, or until the next contract is negotiated by your union. If you are retired, you really know what a " fixed income" is all about.

What happens to your attitude about your income when you give it a title " fixed income?" Do you tend to limit it? Do you hold tight to your purse or pocketbook, or carefully button your hip pocket? /1 Matthew 8.13

1

Do you feel you are taking from someone if you desire more, or you don't deserve to have a greater income, or you are more holy if you are poor?

God is the source of our supply and that includes money. There is no limit except the limit we place upon ourselves by our belief. All of the above excuses are limiting beliefs. You can change your mind. You are not bound by any previous belief. Change it now!

How Strong Is Your Faith?

We are going to talk about faith. Do you say, "I don't have any faith. If I do, it's in Murphy's Law. The worst will always happen." That is negative faith.

Ernest Holmes believed that, "Thoughts are things, and you could change your life by changing your thought."/2 Our minds are like computers, which take reprogramming to change the output. It takes conscious, positive thought, and a lot of it, to change our minds. The best way to increase your faith is to start where you are. Start with the faith you have.

A lady who was in dire financial straits was attending the prosperity workshop. The plan was to go to the laundromat afterwards to wash her clothes. She had been saving money all week. When the clothes were put into the dryer she found twenty dollars. The next week she found ten dollars in the dryer.
/2 SMTB, Holmes, p. 244.2

2

She missed a session of the workshop, and the third week, sure enough, she found no money in the dryer.She began to think it was luck or perhaps our sessions were magical. Of course, neither was correct. By changing her view about money ever so slightly, from lacking to having, she began looking for money and other things she needed as she went about her daily living. The discovery money and other good things were coming to her all the time and in many different ways was new to her. She had never paid any attention.

Pay Attention To God's Gifts

So, pay attention! When money is needed, and you are asking for money, pay attention. Expect it to come and be watchful as to the means.

When money or needed things come to you, always give thanks to the person (the instrument of GOD) and to God the Universal Provider. The energy of giving thanks encourages more of the same pouring into your hands.

God is the source of our supply. There is no limit except the limit we place upon ourselves by our belief. God is always supporting us abundantly. Money, things, whatever our need is God is always giving to us. But we don't pay attention. Money and things are given to us unexpectedly all the time.

Are you expecting it to happen like manna from heaven? Are you expecting the heavens to open up and bring you prosperity? Perhaps, but not

3

always so. Usually, we have no idea from where more money will come. We stand there frozen in desperate confusion.

People are also channels of God's good and we often don't notice all the gifts that come to us on any given day. What about the zucchini your neighbor gave you? Or the love gift you received on Mother's Day? What about the butcher who saved bones for your dog and didn't charge you for them? Did you notice that rebate for overpayment or coupon for your favorite food?

Lucille Ball was reported to have said that, "There is no shortage of anything in this world. There is plenty for all." This is a Principle."God is always causing the rain to fall on the just and the unjust."/3

Prayer Works

Is it time to change your belief? Visualize wells of abundance showering you with money. If your household needs more money function, on picture opening your roof and letting dollars pour into it filling it to the rafters. It won't be long before money will come to you. Affirm, "With God, all things are possible."/4 Rejoice at the mental picture of you paying all your bills at one sitting. Expect it to happen.

A Practitioner friend and his wife shared that on bill-paying day he sat down at his desk and made out the checks. She meanwhile sat in meditation on the abundant supply that God was giving them always. She affirmed that every
/3 Matthew 5.45, /4 Matthew 19.26

bill was paid in full with extra to spare. This always happened. They claimed. They believed that each one of them was doing an important job.

If you don't have a partner to share the task of bill-paying, allow yourself at least fifteen minutes to meditate and affirm God's abundant supply before you start, and give thanks (whatever the outcome) for every bill you could pay. Allow wisdom to guide you. Do not overextend yourself. Pay the bills with the money you have at that time. Listen to your inner voice when it comes to finances. God is always abundantly supplying our every need.

One time we thought it would be beneficial to refinance our home loan. We replied to an advertisement that came in the mail. The loan company was eager to serve us but the rates seemed a little high. On inquiring with the loan managers of the company who held our loan, they thought it too high also. "Would you continue your loan with us if we could match the bid or even give a lower one?" they inquired. "Of course!" was our reply. We were able to keep our loan with our regular company with no points or other fees, no paperwork, and they lowered our interest rate considerably. God works in wonderful ways to provide for those who ask believing.

To begin at the beginning, as we all have to do from time to time whether we are a beginning student or an advanced student of many years experience, if you are not satisfied with the amount of money you get monthly or yearly, it's time to change your belief and build a new faith that God is the source of your supply.

How do you build faith? You start small. For the real beginner, finding money in your path is exciting and faith building. Somehow, having the money to pay that 'big bill' because the money came in for that purpose reinforces that God is the source. For the advanced student, it is revealed when life provides a lifetime income base without worry or care and brings about some of the extras, such as that long-desired vacation or new home. Take one step at a time.

FORMULA:
1. Despite appearances, declare that God is always supporting your every need.
2. Affirm this daily.
3. Expect this to be true.
4. Watch for it. Record it when it happens.
5. Give thanks, whether it has appeared or not.

If you feel you have very little faith, I suggest you do something to change that attitude. The Unexpected/Expected Income Jar is just such an activity that will expand your view and build your faith.

Get a jar that you like the looks of and put this label on it. UNEXPECTED/EXPECTED INCOME CLUB.

It can be used in several ways. Put it on your dinner table where you often sit. Daily put money (if you desire money) into your jar. As your faith increases so will the money coming into you. Make your Contract with the Universe and review it regularly. Each day contribute as much as your faith allows. Visualize your desired outcome. Give expecting to receive. Your subconscious mind will not allow you to accept something for nothing. The Universe conversely will not give you what you are not willing to accept.

UNEXPECTED INCOME CLUB

Contract with the Universe: _Since I am abundantly supplied with every good thing, I will joyfully give of my opulence daily. I will also give 10% of any unexpected income to my church. Therefore, I will be fulfilling my part in the Law of Giving and Receiving._

Signed_____Date_____

Affirm Daily: I know that the Universe (God) is the source of my supply. I know every need I have is supplied at all times. I let go of any idea to the contrary and am thankful. I joyfully await the physical manifestation. *I let go and let God!*

Make copies of this affirmation to carry with you.

THE SEED MONEY PROCESS:
1. Give whatever amount you wish to the jar each day.
2. Bless what you give and affirm a bountiful return.
3. Give what you wish to receive.
4. Expect something wonderful to happen.
5. Do not specify how it is to come about.

Another way to use the Unexpected Income Jar
is to pay attention. God is always providing for
your every need. What about the flowers your
neighbor gave you, or that birthday check your
aunt sent you, or that lunch your friend paid
for? Pay attention and be thankful to God for
these blessings. When Unexpected Income,
things, or services came to you - like the bill to
fix your car was so much less than the bid - you
were ecstatic! All these ways and many more
are the ways God is supplying your every need.
Acknowledge these gifts of God by putting 10%
into your Unexpected/ Expected Income Jar.

The Bible presents many ways to increase your
in-
come, which have to do with giving. Give 10% of
what you wish to receive. Many people say," I
give of my time to the church." Well, if you give
time, you will get time. Is that what you want?"
Do you want money or the things that money
can buy?

Some of us claim we live on a fixed income. The
only place it is fixed is in your mind. If the
Universe-God is always giving to us, but you
believe your Social Security check is all you
have and there isn't any more, that will be the
truth for you. Using the Unexpected/Expected
Income Jar method will explode the 'fixed
income' idea and expand your bank account.

What do you vision when you give to your
church or other charity? Do you think,"Bye,
bye, birdie, never to return," or do you see it
returned multiplied many times? Some people

feel they don't deserve to gain from any gift they give so they put that into the law. And they don't gain at all.

It is said that John D. Rockefeller gave frugally but regularly early in his life. As time went on he increased the percentage of his gifts. He always expected the return on his gifts multiplied many times and it was so. He could not out-give God. He formed the Rockefeller Foundation to give money away.

Will You Tithe Or Give Seed Money, Or Both?

What is the difference between tithe and seed money? Tithe is a gift after you have made your income. This is a universal decree, /5

Seed money is a gift of faith you give to claim your tenfold return.

The Universe knows no difference, large or small, so claim as much as you desire. Why not a million fold? Nothing wrong with that. You have to envision a million fold. You must be able to imagine you already have it. If you doubt it or cannot envision that you will receive even tenfold, you will not. Doubt shuts off the action of the Universe and blocks the return. Whatever you believe the most will be the result. That is why we suggest you give as seed money only the amount you can really envision to have returned to you that day. Then expect it!

Are you ready to change your mind? When you change your mind, you change your belief and it /5 Malachi 3:10.

9

isn't long before you change your experience. As you put 10% of your unexpected income into your jar, repeat the Acknowledgement of God's Provision

Acknowledgement of God's Provision:
I return to the Source-God 10% of the gift that was so generously given to me. Joyously, I give thanks for my continued blessings.

Affirmation for Giving Daily Seed Money:
I affirm that my every need is supplied before I ask and as I pay attention to the source of all Good, all is provided. I let go of any limiting thoughts and rejoice in the blessings of the Universe. Thank you, God!

Remember: If you do not give from you Unexpected/Expected Income Jar for any reason it signals the subconscious mind you are indeed limited and that you do not trust the Universe to supply your needs. This is an important step in faith. Begin today!

Step by step as your faith increases, you will notice that your whole life will become more prosperous Then you will begin to expect unexpected income but never take it for granted. If you do, you will eventually have to prove this Principle again.

<u>DAY BY DAY BUILD A STRONG FAITH THAT</u>

<u>GOD IS THE SOURCE OF YOUR SUPPLY!</u>

Chapter 2

DISCOVERING YOUR MIND SET

Everyone wants to be prosperous. We all desire abundance in our lives. It is true that we each have a different picture of what abundance or prosperity means to us, but basically most people desire to have their needs met with ease and be comfortable in life. Most people don't know how to be prosperous or live abundantly.

We shall begin as if you have no faith at all. Zero! And we shall learn how to build faith. Simultaneously your prosperity level will increase. I assure you it is possible to live comfortably in this world every day of your life.

Start by looking where the true answers lie: inside yourself. For generations we have looked outside at the world in horror at what we saw and it hasn't provided the answer as yet. It is not out there. It is within you.

Start by asking yourself, "What do I think about myself being prosperous?"

Good   Bad   Neutral

Are you afraid to even think of being prosperous? You might be taking something away from someone else, or you might lose your friends or status in your family? Many long held beliefs that are completely untraceable to your present

11

memory have formed the life you are now living.

YOUR PRESENT ATTITUDE IS THE KEY. YOUR PERCEPTION OF A SITUATION IS VITAL. YOUR MENTAL ATTITUDE IS CRUCIAL TO YOUR SUCCESS IN BECOMING PROSPEROUS PERMANENTLY. YOUR ATTITUDE IS THE KEY.

Attitudes are made up of all the beliefs you hold about anything.   What is your attitude about being prosperous?   Ask yourself:
1. Is it OK for others to be prosperous
    but not me?   Yes   No
2. I don't want to be rich.   Yes   No
3. I like my life just the way it is.   Yes   No
4. I have all I need right now.   Yes   No
5. Poor people are God's people.
    It's a blessing to be poor.   Yes   No
6. Greater steps can be made in
    consciousness if you are poor
    or struggling.   Yes   No

What is your attitude?_____
_____
_____

My next question, are you willing to change your mind from negative beliefs to positive ones?   If you are not,   give this book to someone who is ready to change his/her mind. Go no further, as this book will be of little value to you. Are you saying "I tried it and it didn't work"?Your attitude is the key . If you are not willing to change, there will be no change in your life experience.

Discover Your Attitude About Money

It is important to discover what your long-held beliefs are regarding money.   If your belief is that money is the root of all evil, or a corruption,   or any other negative idea other than a simple means of exchange,   then you need to begin by changing your feelings about money.

Our forefathers tried to express a blessing through our money by stamping "In God We Trust " and other such ideas and pictures denoting its divine purpose.

You may need to desensitize yourself by remembering that before money came into fashion, sea shells, deer skins, necklaces, and/or domesticated animals were used as a means of exchange. Are they evil?   Of course not!   Where did we get the idea that money is evil?

The quotation from the Bible,/1 "The love of money is the root of all evil," is often   mis-quoted to read "money is the root of all evil." I do not know anyone who "loves" money. I know many people who really like the life style that money can buy. And there is a difference.

Whatever your attitude is about money, you can change it. So start now. Take out a coin. Look it over. Read its motto. Decide whether it's good
/1   1 Tim.6.10

13

or bad. Take out a bill. Check it out. Decide whether it's good or bad.   Are you willing to accept more of the same   or   of a higher denomination? Desensitize yourself to money. Your attitude is the key, and you can change your experience by changing your attitude.

If your mind does not accept your new ideas at first, do not be dismayed. It took a lifetime to implant your present attitude, so it will take some time to change it. Meanwhile, your mind may not accept your new way of thinking, so diligence is recommended. As we proceed we will suggest mind tricks to change your view of life.

ATTITUDE ABOUT MONEY WORKSHEET
1. Uncover your beliefs about money, circle
   every attitude you hold.
2. Put a star by the positive attitudes.
3. Total at the bottom.

fear of not enough   God is money also
fear of too much   life is hard
blessing   God is the source
curse   abundant
gift of God   plenty
filthy   easy come easy go
unlimited   you have to earn it
lack   free flow
give   stretch that dollar
freely receive   frugal
riches are sinful   limitation
poor are 'God's people'   need more
I don't deserve it.   not enough

poverty
enough for everyone
millionaire, not me
money is bad.
opulence
depression near
wealth
automatic
give, give, give
life is good

almighty dollar
money is God action
Divine Right
weak economy
I am rich
earn a living
save, save, save
inherit riches
given freely
Prosperity Law

Other_____

Total positive_____

Total negative_____Neutral_____

How did you measure up? Some ideas are positive to one person and negative to another. Did you find that you hold more positive ideas concerning money than negative? Good for you!

The items you circled form a picture of your mind set and your beliefs about money.

For each negative mind set, find the opposite or make up an opposite. Write an affirmation using the positive ideas listed.

I affirm that _____

_____
_____
_____
_____

Changing Your Mind-set

You are right. You are about to change your mind or mind-set. Your long-held belief about money and its purpose is what you see in your present experience. A mind-set is neither bad nor good. It is merely a long-held belief, the results of which you get to experience. If you are not satisfied with the result of your mind-set, spend time writing an affirmation for each negative mind-set you uncovered. The new affirmation will have to be spoken, thought consciously, written, and repeated many times before it becomes your new mind-set on the subject of money. Every bit of time spent is well worth it.

Begin now! Your attitude is the key.

Changing Your Attitude

Much has been written about how to change your mental attitude about life and the things of the world. Try listening to a tape made of your own affirmations and/or print them on cards and post them in prominent places in your house. As you go about changing your mind-set on money, start replacing it with an attitude of expectancy, an attitude of expecting money to come. Replacing thoughts of lack has great power and will cause unexpected money to flow into your bank account or pocket.

Be quite specific. Say, "I affirm money for all my

needs, and some to spare is at my disposal, now!" Do not be afraid to use the word money. If you want money, ask for money. An old story is told that a lady affirmed abundance. She got abundance all right: Nine Labrador retriever puppies were born to her dog and five kittens to her cat!

You get what you expect when you ask rightly. Positive expectancy has great power. When you expect the best, you'll get the best.

Even before you begin to experience a change in your supply, start giving thanks for all that you have. Gratitude has power. Say, "THANK YOU, GOD! THANK YOU, UNIVERSE!" Go around your house thanking God for every item, every blessing you have.

Make it a practice: Affirm, expect and give thanks long before your desire materializes. Celebrate when it comes into reality.

God Is The Source

Are you aware you are not the source of your supply, money, or things? Nor is your job, Social Security, or any other material channel. God is the source of all good on this earth. The Universe provides abundantly for every living thing in nature. Why not you and me also? We depend too heavily on the outside world as our source. It fluctuates with the economy, so it is not dependable. Take this quiz and discover some new insights about your source.

QUIZ YOURSELF

1. Who or What is the source of my supply? *God*
2. On what basis am I paid? *I am paid according to my true belief in the value of my work or contribution.*
3. Do I believe I can change the amount of my supply? *It will change according to my belief.*
4. Am I willing to do something to increase my supply? *Willingness to do is a beginning step to having.*
5. Am I open to ideas that will increase my supply? *Everything begins with an idea.*
6. Am I willing to act on an idea of Mind as if it were so? *When we act as if it is so, it becomes the Law and is so.*
7. Is my lack of supply my only lack? *The Law meets all needs. It knows neither large nor small. All requests are alike to It.*
8. Am I willing to give up something in order to get something? *When I give up the belief in lack and limitation, all my desires and needs are met.*
9. Do I trust my inner self to know what is right for me? *The Spirit within knows when a thing is right for me. I trust in Its guidance.*
10. Am I willing to accept a gift? *The Universe is always giving. We must clear out our receivers and accept the gift.*

If some of these ideas are new to you, examine them in the light of the Highest Truth and set about putting them into practice as your mental affirmations.

EXPECT MORE, BE MORE

Ask yourself if you are willing to take that additional training class offered to improve your skills at work. As an employee, it would make you more valued.

What about the idea you had to make life easier, or that invention? Its time has come. The book you wrote or idea for a novel waiting in the back of your mind for your action; act upon them! Sometimes hobbies can be spun into full-time businesses. Some of us have developed skills that are valuable to others, such as visiting the sick, driving someone to the doctor, or pet-sitting for someone. Open more channels for your gifts to come to you.

THINGS I CAN DO TO OPEN MORE AVENUES FOR GENERATING MORE SUPPLY:

Ideas that have lain dormant, hobbies that can be utilized, services for others I can perform, ideas, ideas, ideas.

CREATIVE IDEAS

1._____
2._____
3._____
4._____
5._____

6._____
7._____

SERVICE I AM WILLING TO DO

1._____
2._____
3._____
4._____
5._____

Choose one of these ideas to act upon immediately. Begin with what you have. You can do it! Allow your mind to provide you with the first step. Remember the old saying, "The first step is the hardest." I say, getting the first step figured out is the hardest. Doing it is much easier.

The same place you got the idea is where you will find the beginning step. Clear away any limitations until the idea becomes clear.

Affirm: *I now have a clear idea of the first step to accomplish my idea. With God's help I go about doing it with ease.*

Begin a Spiritual Path Notebook. Record your ideas, date, and enter each step along the way to complete success.

If you are expecting more from the Universal Supply, you must be willing to be more in return. Sort through your 'willing to do' list and find one that you will begin immediately, whether you are paid for it or not. Many a lifetime career began from volunteering, seeing a need, and filling it without regard for reimbursement.

Truly, it is within a new idea that fortunes are made, even if it is just designing a new mouse trap. Ideas are in the very air you breathe. All around you are the means to solve all the problems in this world. When you tune in to the Universal Spirit on a regular basis, you open your mind to a wonderful opportunity. Keep your mind open to utilizing one of these creative ideas in your program of prosperity.

Accepting The Gift

Learn how to accept the gifts of the Universe. Implementing them immediately into your life creates more confidence in the ideas that come through you, generating more and more. This intuitive action causes you to be alert to other possibilities. Opportunities are everywhere about us.

The Universe is an endless source of ideas. As you develop your receptivity to these ideas, your life and the level of world consciousness is enhanced. Listening to the Great Within has great power. All human advancement in this world came about by this means. Develop faith in the Universal Presence. It has the power to supply every need.

* Start Your Spiritual Path Notebook.
Use it to record the ideas you have outgrown and
new ideas that you are putting into practice.
Remember: Keep Records! It builds your faith.

Chapter 3

WHAT'S THE GOOD WORD?

When someone asks you, " How are you, today?" How do you answer, "Great! Very well, thank you! Prosperous!"

Practice answering in short affirmative true statements. I Am statements contain great power, whether they are true or not at any one moment of time. The habit of answering affirmatively brings about positive experience in reality.

"I Am" power is used every day. What is it you say when someone greets you saying, "How are you?" You answer, "I Am" don't you?" What do you usually say after that, " tired, fine, busy, sad, etc?" Do you listen to what you say? You are using the "I Am" Power? Start noticing what your regular answer is. If it is not the real truth about you, then you need to change it.

What's the good word for you today? For several years I asked this question of my students in class as a group or individually when they called on the telephone. It brought out many and varied responses. Some of them were, "I am GREAT!, I am a blessed child of God," "I am a healthy, happy spiritual being." "I am an important part of this universe. I am a pure expression of God." Usually a great big breath was taken, like they were reprogramming their minds to another wave length before they replied. One, however, stayed on her original course, "I'm sick, I'm unhappy, I'm broke and I can't work because it's raining." All but that one enjoyed the exercise immensely. What's the good word for you today? _____

We speak from the heart more than we know. It is impossible for us to conceal our inner thoughts from the world or from the Spirit. Until we learn to use the Power for our benefit we will continue to experience life as the world experiences it.

Affirmations

I am a firm believer in affirmations. I believe that they can change the most dreadful experience to a pleasant one, the most devastating disease to perfect health and bring peace, happiness, and prosperity to anyone's life. All you have to do is say them, see them, hear them, write them, and live as if they are so. The most powerful words are those you say about yourself. When you would have said,"I am sick," change it to, "I am well!" Change, "I am unhappy," to, "I am happy!" Instead of, "I'm tired: the baby kept me up all night," change it to, "I'm refreshed and ready to challenge the day" (and keep that baby awake all day). Perhaps you are experiencing a lack in cash flow just now. "Mike Todd is reported to have said,"I've been broke many times, but, I have never been poor." You don't have to settle for this. Change it completely. Affirm, "I'm prosperous, now and always."

All statements about yourself have power. If you repeat them frequently, you will experience their effect.

Begin by deciding on a particular response that is really true, one you can respond to heartily without thought, something that isn't going to shock your inquirer or label you. Practice with one positive response until it's completely natural. Then branch out. Try another. Have two or three polished and automatic so, if you are working on health that day, you can reply, "Great, I am great!" or " Very well, thank you!" And believe it. These are simple affirmations. This is a fine way to start using affirmations. Metaphysicians should greet each other with, "What's the good word with you today?" instead of, "How are you today?" Start practicing this and you will reap great rewards.

"I AM" STATEMENTS

"I Am statements are useful in defining who you are in Spiritual terms. Every time you say, 'I Am' you are creating an experience for yourself. All words have power, whether we are speaking in English or another language. The greatest power is loosed when we say, "I Am" because we usually follow it with a statement about ourselves. Whether good or bad, it indicates the state of our thinking, our health, or our world as perceived by us at that time.

A friend was telling of his job situation recently when he said, "I am very unhappy there. I dread going to work each morning. I am under such stress I am hardly able to do my work." Was this the truth? Certainly it was the truth as my friend saw it. Whether it was the truth or not, it was affecting his entire world. Many of us have worked in a place where the attitude was very negative.

A few years ago, the principal of my school said, "You have the power to make your experience here at this school what you choose. It can be happy or extremely unpleasant. It can be a place you enjoy coming to or one you dread. The choice is yours. Decide what you want to experience. Talk and act as if it is so." At that time there was great disharmony among the faculty members.

I took his advice. Within that year my attitude and the attitude of the teachers at that school changed. It became a pleasant place to work. As the years went by it became a very tightly knit, happy, supportive family. The most important change was in what people were saying about each other, themselves and the school.

What advice would you give someone who is unhappy in their work?

Try these three steps to change what appears to be a hopeless situation. Try them on relationships at work and at home. This attitude will positively affect your finances and your health.

FIRST: Start saying positive "I Am" statements about yourself and your job whether they are true at that time or not. Say, *"I Am able to do my work very well. I Am a dependable, willing worker. I Am thankful for the many opportunities this job has opened for me. I Am noticing the thoughtful, kind, and friendly attitude expressed to me by everyone."* **Yes!**

SECOND: Look for these positive statements to be true. Look for the evidence.

THIRD: Do not listen to the negative at all. When you enter the door, pull an imaginary plastic bag down over you. You will be able to see and hear and work but allow only positive ideas to enter.

So often it is the habit of workers to bad-mouth the establishment or the management, or to pass around unkind gossip about another employee. Do not allow yourself to get into this endless chain of negation. Let it stop with you. Don't even listen. Change the subject.

Clear Your Mind Of Negative Thoughts

When Ernest Holmes was asked by his students how he went about keeping his mind in the positive mode, he explained this way,"Houses were built with nice, wide front porches in the days of my youth. Most evenings and on Sunday afternoons the family gathered there to chat, sing and enjoy each other's company. They entertained guests there, also. Most houses had fences outlining the front yard, with a gate at the sidewalk. Many people passed our house. Some we invited in, Some we did not. Your thoughts are like that. Some you invite in to your consciousness, and some you do not. You nod and let them pass."

Words of Power

When you have decided to begin using WORDS OF POWER in your daily life, immerse yourself in saying, seeing, hearing, and writing positive words that are meaningful to you. As you read your daily inspirational material, choose a thought for the day. Write it on a 3 x 5 card to carry in your pocket. Pull it out many times during the day to review it in your mind. Bring it into your thought over and over. When you have a few favorite affirmations, make a tape in your own voice to listen to as you jog, exercise or ride to or from work. Speak these positive words as often as possible. Find people of like mind who are practicing the principle.

Your Religious Science Church or Study Group is a fine place to find students working on affirmations. Exchange affirmations and share the demonstrations already occurring in your life as a result of this change in attitude.

Begin writing your own affirmations. What are affirmations? SHORT POSITIVE STATEMENTS IN THE PRESENT TENSE THAT ARE MEANINGFUL TO YOU. A good way to start is with I AFFIRM_____ .
You can do it. Affirmations in your own words have meaning to you and are more powerful than other people's ideas.

I Am Power

On the Spiritual Level you will discover who and what you are. Here are some "I AM" AFFIR-MATIONS that define you in the highest degree. Memorize them so that you will have them with you wherever you go.

"I AM" AFFIRMATIONS
Rev. Alyce Bartholomew Soden

I AM a powerful Spiritual Being.

I AM perfect in body, mind, and spirit.

Love is the cornerstone of all my happy and
harmonious human relationships.

I AM abundant, pressed down and running
over.
I AM ONE WITH THE UNIVERSE

I suggest you commit these statements to
memory. Having an affirmation in your memory
that has the power to bring you to your center is
a beginning step in taking charge of your life.

Any one of these Truths will do this in case of
need. Our Study Group frequently began the "I
Am" affirmations with the words, "Come to
Center." A lady member of our Study Group was
seriously injured in an automobile accident. On
the gurney awaiting a long transport in an
ambulance to the nearest hospital, one of the
attendants whispered to her,"Come to center."
This triggered these statements in her mind. Her
mind then repeated them again and again. She
was able to remain conscious and pain-free on
her most uncomfortable journey.

How many exposures to a new idea does it take
to change your belief in something?   It takes
many exposures on all levels as your six senses

will attest. Be patient with yourself but persist. Unlearning takes time and perseverance. <u>You can do it!</u>

A bountiful harvest of grapes or olives is said to be "pressed down and running over" the press.

Chapter 4

VISIONING

Try this experiment: without looking in your pocket or purse, bring to mind the money you have on your person. Is that all you have? Think savings account, checking account or other liquid assets. We carry a money ledger in our mind, a vision of every penny we have.

Next, account for every bill you owe. How much money could you spend this minute for something you really want or need?

Notice the mental gymnastics you just went through. You are a walking spreadsheet of your financial status every moment.

The information of how much money a person has in his/her purse, wallet, or bank account is quite common. Usually, your mind contains how much is coming in and how it is to be spent. There is nothing wrong in this. However, along with this knowledge often is an opinion that limits the cash flow. This could be called 'money talk.' The mental accounting of the money you have flowing through your hands does give an impression of more than enough or not enough. Impressions held for any length of time will begin to be self-fulfilling.

How do you discover what mental attitude you have been generating? Look at your life situation. Is it filled with abundance, beautiful homes, fine cars, stylish clothes, and money to do the things you desire? Or do you see lack and limitation in every direction? The effect of your mental attitude is directly reflected into your world.

Another way to discover your mental attitude is when some unexpected money comes into your hands, what is your 'money talk' about it? Do you hold on to it as if there isn't any more coming? Do you pay off that most pressing bill to relieve the pressure of limitation? Do you give yourself a treat, buy that long desired object? Most people do a little of each. 'Money talk' is that which goes on in your decision-making process. Pay attention to why you choose one plan over another. Planning to stretch that money because it appears that's all there is for you, is an attitude of lack and limitation. It is a feeling that the world out there is not going to generate any more money for you so you had better make this go as far as possible. This limits the possibilities of more coming from the outer world.

I need, I need, I have, I have!

What do you pay attention to when you need something? You pay attention to that need. Yes! When you spend time contemplating 'needing,' you are going to keep right on 'needing.' The more you say, "I need a mate, I need $20.00," "I need new shoes," "I need...." and so on to infinity, needing becomes the truth about you. You will go through life needing 'things" or wanting 'things. I'm not telling you that you don't need 'things.' I am showing you a new way of getting what you want and need. Some people believe they should not want things. My belief is that all things are expressions of God providing for our use. Not to want these things to use would be to deny their purpose in our lives.

Are you coming from viewing the cup half full instead of half empty? The Principle goes like this: that to which you give your attention grows and multiplies. Good or not good is not the question. There is no judgment of the value, big or little, bad or good. God creates through you that to which you give your attention. The things you contemplate become the law of your life. The choice is yours. You can think about needing or having. You can think about poverty or plenty.

What pictures come to your mind when you say "I need," poverty or plenty? The more you affirm poverty is the truth for you, the more you will experience poverty. When you affirm plenty on the other hand, the Universe sets about making that the truth for you, through you. And the things you list that you do not have to fulfill this picture, are provided. Affirm prosperity and feed your mind with thoughts of being prosperous. Cooperate with the Principle of Prosperity. Use it. Affirm that you have your desire and you will have it. This is the easiest way to live a prosperous life. If you keep saying "I need, I need, I need, I need," YOU WILL!

Start saying: "I HAVE, I HAVE, I HAVE, Thank you God!" And you will have a life of unbounded prosperity.

I'd Rather Be Sailing

Do you pay off one creditor and find yourself back in that same situation a few months later? It's time to review your spending pattern on the physical level and the mental anxiety it causes. You may not see yourself as debt free. Your mind may be set in the, "I owe, I owe, I owe. So off to work I go," mode or circle. You may need to examine why you work. Is it just to pay the bills? Now is the time to examine your mental attitude about your work and its purpose in your life. Ask yourself these questions:

1. Do I like my work? _____

_____

2. Is my work rewarding in other ways than the salary I bring in?_____

_____

3. If I had my choice Id' be _____

_____

4. What can I do today towards making my work the most pleasant, exciting place to be ?

_____

_____

_____

Looking at your reaction to these four questions is sometimes self-revealing. My method is to start where you are and make it the best, rather than chucking the whole thing and running away to Shanghai. Most people who run away from a situation take that situation plus more with them and discover the same wherever they go. You have seen this happening in others.It may be happening in your life as well.

This reminds me of an old story: An old man was resting by the side of the road. A young man coming along decided to restalso. Viewing the town in the distance the young man inquired, "Are you from around here?" The older man nodded affirmatively. "What are the people like in the town ahead? Are they good, kind, loving, and giving?" he asked. Instead of answering the question, the older man asked, "What kind of people lived in the town you came from?" "They were mean and selfish." answered the younger man. "That is the kind you will find here," replied the older man.

Using your positive ideas to improve the situation where you are is the place to start. Plan to make the place you are in the very best.

Action and Visualization

Sometimes it takes strong measures to break the 'in debt" pattern of action. Decide today on a plan to break this pattern in your life. If you have to cut up all your credit cards, do it! Credit cards may be a blessing to some people, but definitely not all. Take your stand. Stay within your budget.

Visualize yourself as debt free. How would you feel? See that satisfied smile on your face when you pay cash for that large item for which you have saved. Make this a goal: be debt free and pay cash for your next car or house or vacation.

What is the difference between goal setting and following your inner vision? If you are attuned with the Infinite Spirit as the source of your supply lifetime and have committed your way to the higher path, it may well be they are the same. As you expand in consciousness, your vision becomes your goal and your goal becomes your vision

Chapter 5

VISUALIZE YOUR DESIRES

CARTOON
I have used this cartoon drawn by my friend
Mindy Eisman to assist me in increasing my
business. I keep it posted over my desk. My
Coast Wedding Service utilizes the telephone
greatly. I keep it posted over my desk and when I
haven't received a call lately, I look at it closely
and enjoy the feeling expressed by getting a
bunch of money coming into me from telephone
reservations.

Where does money come from? Is it solely as a
result of your efforts? Or are you waiting to
hear that your rich uncle has died and left you a
fortune or that you won the 60 million dollar
Lottery jackpot.

Truly, money is not generated from the outer world. It is a gift of God. It is the result of the vision about money that you contain within you. And of course, most of us do not desire money for money's sake, but for that which money can buy. Money is only paper and metal. It is not necessarily prosperity. Freedom from lack, all needs supplied that we desire, these desires can be fulfilled without any money being involved. However, we do live in this world, and money is the common means of exchange.

God does not demand any particular action from us. Whether we are prosperous or not in this lifetime is a result of our choices. We choose as we grow in spiritual awareness and as we learn to use the Principles. Each person chooses this, or his/her own pathway, so no one is really ahead of any other person.

If you are having difficulty visioning unlimited supply, start paying attention to the 'money talk' that you allow to shape your experience with money. Can you visualize yourself driving that beautiful new car or living in that spacious new home filled with new furnishings? Can you see your bank account in six figures, money coming in and out, but never less than six figures.

What Is Your Conditioning About Money?

We have been so conditioned to the idea that the worship of money is the root of all evil,we feel tainted when money comes to us, particularly money we haven't worked for. We tend to feel hesitant about using it for our good purposes. Sometimes we feel we don't deserve it. When money comes to you, be grateful to God for supplying all your needs. Thank God, the source of all good, and thank the physical source as well. The Universe is always providing all for Its creation's needs.

Dreams do come true. A young family dreamed of living in the 'Little House on the Prairie' mode. It is quite a task to find such a place near the city with the modern world of freeways and housing tracts. They enjoyed outings on the weekends in the forested areas. One time they took a different route and found an old small cabin for sale with trees and a stream running through the property. This was exactly what they wanted and the Universe provided. The challenges were many. First, they had to fix up and sell their house in the city, then get financing - no easy task on a hundred-year-old cabin in a forested area. As this was all taking place, the father lost his job. A few months later when he got a new job it was nearer their cabin. They began living their dream.

Isn't that what we all want, to live our dream? How do we go about it?

1. Clear away any beliefs that you can't live your dream.
2. Get a clear picture of exactly what you want in your mind.
3. Stay with that picture and develop it into the life you want to live.
4. Pay attention. The Universe will supply your dream when you are least expecting it.

39

5. Do what it takes to make it your reality (honorably, of course).
6. PATIENCE ! PATIENCE ! PATIENCE !

When your dream comes true, be grateful to God for supplying all your needs. Thank God, the Source of all good, and thank the physical source also. You are continually abundantly supplied.

Visioning was recorded at least twice in the ministry of Jesus of Nazareth: when He fed the five thousand and later the four thousand /1 and /2. The two incidents happened similarly. After a lengthy time of inspirational teaching in the desert, the Master and the Disciples were concerned about the people. The Disciples suggested sending them to a nearby town to buy food. The Master called for the food that was available, and it was a few loaves and small fish. Instead of sending them away, He took the loaves and fish, blessed them, broke them into pieces, and set them before the multitude. Everyone ate to their fill with baskets left over.

Later when the Master and the Disciples boarded a boat to travel to Bethesda. The Disciples had forgotten to bring enough food, only one loaf of bread for all /3. But Jesus knew it and said to them, "What are you thinking because you have no bread? Do you not even yet know, and do you not understand? Is your heart still hard? You have eyes, and yet do not see? You have ears, and yet you do not hear? And do you not remember? When I broke five loaves of bread for /1 Mark 6.35, /2 Mark 8.14, /3 Mark 8. 17-21

40

the five thousand, how many full baskets of fragments did you take up?" They said to him, " Twelve." He said to them, "And then the seven for the four thousand, how many baskets of fragments did you take up?" They said to Him, "Seven." He said to them, "How is it then that even yet you cannot understand?"

I believe that He was referring to the Principle of Abundance. God is always providing for Its creation, abundantly. All we have to do is ask believing and accept the blessing.

Do you think He really saw just a few loaves and fishes? When He blessed them, He saw food for everyone present and plenty to spare. He visualized what He wanted, gave thanks to God for it, and it was so. He broke it into pieces. Every person who manages the kitchen at a potluck demonstrates this principle to some degree.

Try the Principle of Abundance with the money you have in your pocket or purse right now. Take it into your hands as a symbol of what you want multiplied. Visualize what you want or need. And bless what you have in your hands knowing that God multiplies ten-,twenty-, or more fold. Then give of that return to your church. At first, it may not seem to be working but as you develop your faith in the Principle, the return will increase. It does not say that Jesus did not eat of the bounty Himself, so take what you need and pass the basket on.

What is Your View of Life?

When the basket of life is passed to you, do you see it filled with delectable morsels or half full of passable food if you are hungry enough? Or, do you see an empty basket filled only with the fruits of your labors? Your view of life is important because what you believe to be true for you will be your experience. It is wonderful that we can always change our view and by so doing we will change our life. Look about you. Nature is a great example of abundance. All the action of nature is governed by Natural Law. There is no shortage or inaction. Even when man interferes in the chain, he just becomes a part of it.

Perhaps your vision of you and your life is too limited. Is it time to expand to a greater view of yourself and your abilities? Who are you? Give the highest answer you can conceive.

WHO ARE YOU? *I am a powerful spiritual being and the Kingdom of Heaven is my home now, not in some future time, but now, right where I am in this place. I am unique and indispensable to the evolutionary experience of humanity.*

Each and every person who lives or has ever lived is also of the royal household and has participated in mankind's journey from God to God.

If you think you don't know what your purpose is in this lifetime, then demonstrating these Principles of Abundance, Increase, and Distribution exemplified by the Master Jesus are the steps for you to begin in your mastery of this world. Your conscious mind may not be aware of the lesson you need to learn or the path you have chosen to follow. What is your next step? Learn to demonstrate God's Grace.

God is blessing you always with all that is good and wonderful and beneficial to you. Your subconscious mind knows this and is ready to assist you on your next step in proving it to your conscious mind by demonstrating these Truths in your physical world. The reason you have not done all this before is that your conscious mind has been in a state of confusion, which we all have to some degree. It is like static on the radio. It distorts our vision of who we are and what we are to learn in this lifetime.

If your vision of yourself is of a poor, limited human being living in a world of sin, sickness and death, subject to the whims of fortune, the caprice of the world, you will experience life in that manner. Remove yourself today from that low level. Acknowledge your high estate. Wield the Power of the Universe that is at your disposal.

We knew it was time to start planning for our retirement home. We really didn't know what we wanted, but we knew it was time. As we traveled on vacation we paid attention to whether we liked a place or not. So, seventeen years before we retired, we sat down and made a list of the kinds of things we liked to do and had envisioned doing when we retired. I like to garden; some acreage would be needed. My husband likes to do woodworking, have a shop and, work with machinery.   He also likes to paint. I like music and writing books.

All these sorts of things we took into account. Maybe we could find a place that doesn't get too hot in the summer or cold in the winter. We looked in Florida,   Colorado,   and near our home in California.   The beach or the desert, which one?   We decided to look at the beach. Starting at the Mexican border we searched on our summer vacations.   Some ideas began to form. Beach property on the water with trees. Perhaps property with electric power and water already improved. A tall order.

One   summer   we   were   touring   Northern California and stopped to enjoy the ocean view. In front of us was a peninsula.   Why not there? We stopped at the next town asking about that property. It had just come up for sale. We visited with the owner and explored it. It seemed just exactly what we wanted,   but at that moment we had no money to put down on it.

Our vision came into focus: that property or something better.

We returned home, deciding to put a bid on that property.   As money became available, we did. But problems began to occur with the property. And the more we researched the matter, the more we knew t it was not for us. However, we began a forced savings that year and saved over $10,000.   Our vision was near the ocean and some acreage,   already improved with water and power and warm,   sheltered from the wind.

The next summer we returned to the area, got a different realtor, and looked at property. One place in particular on that cold and windy day was warm, had beautiful trees and an ocean view. The house that had been there had burned down the year before so the property was discounted. We researched it thoroughly. It had a well, electric power, and maybe a usable septic system. We put the money down and, before escrow was closed, had leveled off a pad to park our motor home.

Visioning often takes the form of an investigation, a moving of the feet, an inner examination and matching of the inner picture. But when you see it, you usually know it on all levels. We did. It was as if we were on a magic carpet. All things came together for our vision to be a reality. Also, we didn't give up just because the first choice did not materialize. We kept on preparing ourselves for success.

By the very clarity of the vision, the action unfolds. This is what is meant by, "The force is with you." When the vision is clear, nothing else can be the result.

What are you desiring or dreaming in your life? Get such a clear picture in your mind that you can see it, feel it, touch it, live it; then it will become a reality for you, also.

Chapter 6

THE POWER OF TREASURE MAPPING

CARTOON: Organize your dreams.

Most people have dreams, desires and needs. Some people have difficulty organizing them and following some kind of plan to put them into action. They appear to be just pipe dreams and, when they come to mind, they negate them immediately with reasons why they will never be nd they l never become reality. Are you ready to make your dreams, desires, and needs become a reality? Treasure Mapping is for you

Do not look out at your world and see impossibilites. To begin, let your limiting ideas go and list your <u>5 greatest needs</u>:

1. _____

2. _____

3. _____

4. _____

5. _____

Be creative. List your 5 greatest desires: (some may overlap).

1. _____

2. _____

3. _____

4. _____

5. _____

Dream a little and list your greatest dreams.

1. _____

2. _____

3. _____

4. _____

5. _____

If you need more space start a notebook. Date each entry.

FIRST: prioritize them for your greatest needs, desires, or dreams, now.

SECOND: analyize them for similarities. Are

some related to each other?

THIRD: prepare them for your Treasure Map.

Your inner eye knows what is needed and desired. If you use pictures cut from magazines, this will help lead to the symbol of your dream. Treasure Mapping helps clarify the vision and provides constancy of purpose that may be difficult for a beginner. Often we have wonderful ideas, but we cannot visualize them or focus our mind consistently on them so they never materialize. Prayerfully make your Map using all levels of intuition. Review it regularly and keep a log on the events as they occur. Your goal will become a reality. Review your Map giving thanks to God for this blessing. As each part unfolds, rejoice.

As your need, desire, and dream become a reality, one by one, your confidence will increase and your faith in God's all givingness to Its Divine Children becomes magnified.

To begin, you need to decide which graphic form is most suitable to your purpose. A chart for a single item or notebook for your life plan.

Poster: wheel ideas on one theme
                     collage of ideas
Notebook: each page for a subject
Road map: life goals (excellent for guiding
                     childrens' values and academic
                     goal-setting program)
Ladder Design: A sequence of Events
                     High School Graduation,
                     College Graduation,

job, marriage, children, etc.

See illustrations on p.51
Wheel,Roadmap & Ladder

It helps to begin with an end goal in mind; however, that is not mandatory. A beginning Map could include all areas of life and an affirmation, such as:

1. PERFECT HEALTH: Containing pictures of yourself in perfect health with affirmations thanking God that this is the Truth for you,now! Affirmation: *I affirm that my body is strong, in perfect balance, and suitable for my needs.*

2. ABUNDANCE OF ALL GOOD THINGS, INCLUDING MONEY: Pictures of the things that mean living a prosperous life to you, thanking God also that this is your life experience. Affirmation: *I affirm that I am abundantly supplied with every good thing that I need. All my bills are paid on time with plenty to spare and to share.*

3. HAPPY AND HARMONIOUS RELATIONSHIPS IN ALL AREAS OF YOUR LIFE: Include your family, friends, work associates, and all whom you meet knowing that love goes before, revealing love as your experience, and these blessings follow you every step you take. Affirmation: *I affirm that all my relationships are a blessing to all concerned and whereever I go, love preceeds me, is my automatic reaction, and follows me.*

4. SUCCESS IN ALL YOUR ACTIVITIES: Thank God and yourself for making your life work

49

successfully (OK to recognize your part in this demonstration of the Power). Affirmation: *I affirm that I am successful in all my endeavors. I am fulfilled and blessed.*

5. HIGHER STEPS IN CONSCIOUSNESS are the key to all the aforementioned areas. Know that God is working out Its purpose through you and your pathway to higher consciousness is assured. Affirmation: *I affirm that I am open to God's love and wisdom at all times.*

Sample
Treasure Map

**God is abundantly supplying all my needs
I am healthy, strong, loving, successful and
peaceful. Thank you! Thank you Universe!**

Wheel,

KEEPING MY LIFE ON TRACK

The Ladder
Treasure Map

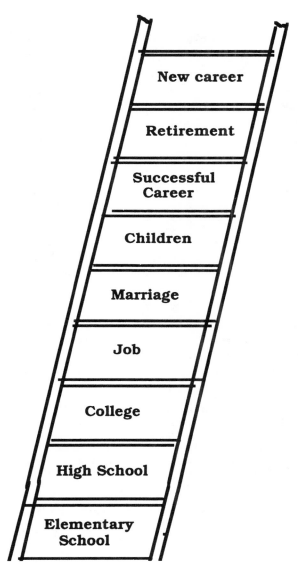

New career

Retirement

Successful
Career

Children

Marriage

Job

College

High School

Elementary
School

Chapter 7

ALL THINGS ASK BELIEVING

If perfect physical health is the subject of your Map, the area of your body that is needing attention can be used as your focus. Find pictures in medical books of the perfect organ or part of the body in question. After focusing on the spine that had been damaged, I was able to become pain free and the body healed itself. I ASKED BELIEVING.

A young friend was told by his Medical Practitioner that, as a result of a knee injury, he would probably be disabled and in a wheel chair before he was thirty and he must not continue to live an active life. But he loved the outdoors, hiking and canoeing were his favorite.

We asked him to draw his knee joint that was in question. He did so from memory as it had been explained to him. Calcium deposits had ground down the edges of his knee bones until they were rounded off. He was in excruciating pain. The picture of the injured knee was well etched in his mind. We found a diagram of a perfect knee joint in a medical book, and he was instructed to practice drawing that picture over and over until it was automatic. Surgery was planned some three months away. During that time, we focused our attention on the perfect knee drawing knowing that his knee was without blemish, completely functioning and pain free.

The time for the surgery arrived and was put off

as his pain had lessened. We continued seeing that perfect knee as his knee. Two things occurred: first, a new medical procedure was discovered that was not as debilitating as the previous surgical method. Instead of cutting the entire knee open to scrape the bone, a vacuum was introduced through a small opening to clean up the calcium. Second, much to the doctor's surprise there was very little calcium to vacuum and the x-rays showed the bone growing back to its normal shape. The doctor's verdict, "Go and enjoy life." He has had no pain in that knee since When we began praying for his complete healing, it seemed impossible but our belief prevailed.

Picture Success

They say a picture is worth a thousand words. This is true when the picture we carry for many years is that we are failures, lazy, bad, not responsible, quitters, or any other expression of low self-esteem. Change that picture. Collect pictures of winners, successful people doing the thing that has made them famous. If you desire to be a dancer, collect pictures of famous dancers. If being a virtuoso pianist or violinist is your desire, collect pictures of famous musicians. Include your own picture among them, doing the thing you do best. Change the picture you hold of yourself. See yourself as a success, a winner.

There is an old tale called "The Ugly Prince" that exemplifies this completely.

Once upon a time a king and queen were

expecting their first child with joy and thanksgiving. When the prince was born, instead of more joy as they had expected, there was great sorrow as their son was ugly, so ugly that the doctor ran away in horror, the nurses fainted, and the parents did not know what to do. Finally, they decided to hire a blind man to care for him, and they built a castle a little bit away from the palace for him to live. The child grew into a quiet sort. On the prince's birthday each year, the king would visit him and ask what he would like as a present. When he was five, he wanted a pony. At six, a building set.

At seven, much to the king's dismay he wanted a statue built of the most handsome man in the kingdom. He himself was to select the model. Standing behind a screen, the prince looked at each young man as he was presented. Finally, he chose a handsome and kind shepherd lad. The statue was made. At the prince's command the statue was placed on a pedestal in his garden. The prince spent many hours looking at his statue. As the years went by, the king noticed on his yearly visits that his son was not as ugly as before. He even remarked to the queen that either he was getting used to his son's appearance, or he was changed. Finally, on the boy's his eighteenth birthday, the king proudly presented his son to the kingdom. He looked amazingly like the statue in his garden.

If you believe that you can't change your looks or any part of your body, that will be the truth for you. But if you believe that you can, use this form of picturing, and it will change.

Relationships

A young man decided he wanted a girl friend. He made his Map in a chart form and pasted a picture of the girl of his dreams on it. He neglected to mention matching similar moral values, education, kind of life style, and spiritual interests to his own. He got the girl on his map physically, but in no way were they similar otherwise, to his sad experience after they were married.

Be cautioned that putting some well-known personage on your Map does not assure that person will come into your life. Always, the person's right of free choice is honored.

A widowed woman decided that she desired a husband. She sat down and made a list of the attributes she most appreciated in a man. She found a picture of a man who exemplified those attributes. In a chart form she put the picture at the top and printed the words best describing him below: home-loving, companion, handy with tools, enjoys classical music, financially well off, active in sports, etc.

Daily she reviewed her Treasure Map, especially the parts of giving thanks to God for this blessing. The more she studied this man she was depicting, the more she realized that she was not the type to attract this kind of person. She then studied herself and realized she would have to change. If she desired a man who was home loving, she would have to become a home lover, also. So, looking around her house, she decided to make some changes. She decided to learn how to cook. She practiced on the church potluck dinners. Every time she made something special she noticed if any one went back for seconds particularly if a man took seconds. She accumulated a number of special recipes that appealed to men. But it was the home made bread that was the clincher. One time she brought homemade bread to the potluck.

One man in particular paid attention to that 'delicious bread.' He made a point of introducing himself and it wasn't long before they were married. She realized that she had to be greater to attract someone greater.

Over the period of time, she also looked at her appearance, her manner of looking at the world, and etc. She was not at all the same widow woman who began the Treasure Map to attract a husband. This woman was willing to change and ask believing and it came to pass.

Illustrations: wheel and ladder

Harmonious Relationships

Estrangement in families is so distressing. Treasure Mapping can be a means to end estrangement in your family.

In chart form or on a page in your notebook put a picture or simulated picture (picture that reminds you) of the persons who are at odds with each other. If this includes yourself, put your picture there. Write affirmations of love and peace around the pictures such as: God's love is permeating each person in this situation, bringing about a loving relationship. Heal this situation by using a pink crayon mark, encircling the group in lovely pink energy, or paste it on pink paper. Thank God daily for this blessed healing. It works!

What about at work? If there is unhappiness at your work, get a picture of your colleagues or find a picture of a group of people working happily together. Put this on your Map. Name the various people if you like. Surround them with positive affirmations and much thanksgiving to God for the fine, harmonious associations of love and cooperation abounding.

Illustration: Road map

Success

So often I read that you are truly the measure of your own success. This is true in the highest sense as we do live in the world. The measure of success in the world is money, power, expertise, or prowess in your chosen field. However, success means something different to each of us. Isn't it wonderful that we are not all trying to succeed in the same field.

Preparation is always the key. I believe there is no substitute for being prepared with the skills needed to be successful. "I paid my dues!" is often said by someone who meteorically raises to fame or fortune. All successful people pay in some form for their acclaim. The price is too high for others.

A positive attitude goes a long way as you prepare yourself for your chosen profession. Also, the determination and stick-to-itiveness to overcome the obstacles (usually of our own making) and continue on your vision is vital. A Treasure Map is most helpful in this area.

What have you been dreaming of doing in this life? This question is valid at any age or time in life, whether you are just starting out or have been about for some time. Usually, the question immediately triggers a mental response. If it does not, begin asking it as you doze off to sleep at night. Keep records of your first thoughts on awakening. The inner you knows the answer.

Let's face it, setting out in life with a plan has much greater prospects than with no plan at all. Parents who hold great expectations for their children and help them prepare for life are often rewarded by seeing them manifested.

Any plan set into motion believing that it will happen is bound to succeed.

Chapter 8

BEGIN TREASURE MAPPING TODAY!

So your dream is to be _____.
Search through the magazines for pictures
resembling yourself doing exactly that. Paste
them on yellow paper of expectancy and
revelation. Place words describing exactly what
your dream is about. Edge the paper with
affirmations that this is the reality for you, now!
Include statements thanking God for this
blessing. All the while continue to prepare in
every way that is revealed to you. Your dream
will come true.

Abundance of Every Good Thing

Treasure Mapping is very useful in getting
things. And there is nothing wrong with that.
Treasure Mapping was first discovered by my
mother, Stella Bartholomew in a Unity
publication in 1928. She began using it
immediately. I remember that she had the first
electric refrigerator on her block, the first
automatic washing machine in our
neighborhood, and many other firsts. Her
Treasure Map showed big X's on the pictures
over and over. When an item was hers in reality
she X'd it out, but left the picture as a
reminder.

Money ! What about money? Treasure Mapping
is well known for generating cash money. A
picture of a thousand dollar bill on your Map
will generate thousands of dollars if you believe
that it is possible. God does not know big or

little, cars, trees, or money. What you put in your Treasure Map believing will be so. Stay open to expected and unexpected money. Believing that it can only come from one source is limiting.

The lottery! What about winning the lottery? My question to you is, "Why haven't you won it before now?" Because you believe that the odds are against you? As long as you hold that to be true in any area of your life, it will be.

The Purpose of Treasure Mapping

The Purpose of Treasure Mapping is to change your belief from not having to having. Anything you put your attention to believing will come to pass. Even winning the lottery. Keep in mind that most people who do win the lottery find themselves back in the same circumstances as they began a few short years before. For permanent prosperity you need to make your Map affirming freedom from lack and limitation in this lifetime.

Be specific in your design. If you desire a car, place a picture of the exact make, model, and color on your Map. A friend put a picture of a new white Oldsmobile sedan with a white interior on her Map. A few weeks later her husband brought home exactly that same car and gave it to her. He had not seen her Map.

I have discovered , if you change your mind, you had better remove that picture from your Map immediately or you will have that item whether you want it or not. Carpeting comes to mind.

After looking for carpeting I found some I liked and brought home a sample. (2 X 2 inch square), to put on my Map. A few days later I found another I liked better, but forgot to remove the first sample. The second choice became no longer available and I found nothing close to it. In the end, I took the carpet that I had originally put on my Map.

It became time for us to build our house on our property as retirement was only seven years away. Each summer we had enjoyed spending our vacations there and improving the property. After designing our house, we searched for an architect and an engineer for our retaining wall, but to no avail. We also needed financing. The property was in a remote area and all the lending institutions were skeptical. As the plans took shape we placed them on our Treasure Map, affirming all needs were met to make this home a reality. Step by step, it became a reality. A company that was willing to stress our plans, (redraw our plans to scale with all the building code requirements,engineering, and architectural seal) and also had a kit house with a similar floor plan. They were able to use their engineering and calculations. Very little change had to be made, except for room size. Since this was a passive solar home, a great number of heat-loss calculations were required. A local lender agreed to finance our project. So, we began.

I would be lying to you if I said that all was smooth sailing and uneventful. I guess I believed that building a house has to be difficult.

When the precut house was delivered on two forty-foot trucks, stacks and stacks of lumber and other building materials were dropped in our front yard.

We also discovered that day that our contractor had moved out of the area, just left. We had to find another contractor but none was available.

With winter rains coming - between 45 and 60 inches annually we had to build the basement ourselves and store the remaining building materials in it for the winter.

Many credits go to my dear, skilled husband. He and our faithful tractor always seemed to know what to do and how to do it.

During the winter, we Treasure Mapped every detail of our house. As a result, a fine dependable contractor was found and,by spring, the watertight shell became a reality.

That year, there was a drought all over California. Our sources of water dried up. We added abundance of water to our Map. Within weeks of our completing the house, city water was brought to our door.

Did I mention that we ran out of money in the middle of the project? And getting a loan on a house in progress is considered impossible. We held to the picture of our dream coming true. It seemed we called every loan company in the state. Finally, a loan company with whom we had done business for many years came to the rescue. Many items that were needed were given

64

to us or we bought at extremely reduced prices. Over and over the Universe provided. Whatever we needed, we had it at the right time and usually in a wonderful way.

Our dream house is completed now and we are living joyfully and happily in it. Thank You, God!

Photograph: Our house under construction.

Chapter 9

TREASURE MAPPING WITH CHILDREN

I often recommend that parents make a picture map of goals and desires for their children. Starting before birth with perfect body, peaceful and happy disposition, and the like. Parents have successfully Mapped their expected child many times. Parents placing a picture of a newborn on the Treasure Map has brought amazing results. The picture resembled that child at birth.

My mother made a Treasure Map for my brother and myself when we were very young. She described loving, caring, and trustworthy; and included, health, protection, values, and wisdom. Other attributes such as success at school, friends, development of a pleasing personality, generosity, thoughtfulness of others, organized thinking, reliability, and opportunity to experience recognition in our areas of expertise. Because we were metaphysicians, a strong faith and practicing belief in God's loving kindness and direction were included. Patience, peace of mind, and searching for our path was important.

She used a Treasure Map to focus on the high attributes she desired for her children. Looking at how my brother and I turned out, I'd say she was successful.

You may have noticed that most of the attributes put on my Treasure Map were quite general in nature. They would be acceptable for anyone.

How does a parent know in what area their child will excel? It is an Asian custom to place the baby on the floor at his first birthday surrounded by objects representing a number of professions. What the child notices first is carefully noted. He is then educated in that direction. Children often come into life knowing what they are to do and show abilities in that area at an early age.

Mother's Treasure Map for me proved to be very accurate though I was not aware of it until I was an adult. She was quite secretive about it all. Only once or twice did she share her map with me, and then only the things that had come to pass.

I was depicted in cap and gown graduating several times. I remember the picture of a girl standing in front of a microphone singing. As it turned out, I was speaking instead. Family harmony was depicted, and being surrounded by beautiful things in life, too. Levels of consciousness were shown in pictures of the Master Jesus, candles, Bibles, and other inspirational symbols.

Children enjoy making their own Treasure Maps. I suggest that, under adult direction, they focus on developing positive attitudes of themselves as Divine Children of God capable in all areas of their lives. Limit their picturing of desired objects to one at a time. If you do not share their desire, such as your daughter desires a horse and you live in the city, leave it open at the top, by saying "this or something better". You do not know all the possible ways that this can be brought about successfully. She may get the opportunity to work in a riding stable after school for riding lessons. Stranger things have happened.

Can you picture your desires? Your child can imagine his desire in color. Finding colored pictures in magazines that depict his dream helps him become specific. Children should be encouraged to draw. Pictures help the mind mold the substance for our greatest good into reality.

We speed up the action of our desire by picturing it. The picturing method is not limited to physical things but is very helpful in goal setting, like graduating from school, improved health or physical healing, as well as family harmony, and assisting in overcoming bad habits such as nail biting and bed wetting.

For more information about Treasure Mapping with children read, *Parenting the Enlightened Child*, by Alyce Bartholomew Soden.

Chapter 10

USING YOUR TREASURE MAP

Going through life hoping with vague, indefinite goals is not very convincing to the subconscious mind. A clear picture of our greatest desire produces a positive effect, and the Universe tends to honor that picture in reality.

What happens when you use your Treasure Map? The pictures or ideas viewed regularly create a pattern in the mind. Attitudes are developed about ourselves, our bodies, our relationships, our work, and our purpose that shape our view of life.

The Universe always says' "Yes" to whatever we have impressed in our mental pattern and produces it in like kind.

This method of focusing your mind is really not difficult. All you have to do is review your Treasure Map until your mind believes that it is possible for you to do, be, or have your dream. At that point you have come a long way - from impossible to possible. The next step, that it's probable you will have it, is quite easy. By that time, I know that I have it, am doing it, or being it the automatic next step.

Any one who is serious about making a change in their life can do it. TRY IT!

Summary

Steps to making a Treasure Map:

1. Sort out your greatest desires. Ignore how impossible some may seem at this moment. If they are for your good and the good of others, go for them.

2. Find pictures that represent your desire. Also, find statements and/or pictures that glorify God. Positive affirmations are an important part.

3. Paste them on a poster or notebook page. Use any of the aforementioned plans or create your own.

4. Spend time each day in meditation using your Treasure Map to guide your mind from one blessing to another, thanking God all the way.

5. Say, see, and know that your greatest desires are becoming a reality now always in the present tense.

6. Expect your desires to materialize immediately. And be patient until they do. The more you believe the sooner your dream will materialize.

7. Caution: What you put on your Map, believing, you will have, and change your mind, take it off immediately.

8. Do not be concerned with the HOW it is to be done. That's God's business.

Treasure Mapping assists you to identify and receive your greatest desire. All levels of consciousness are used to bring your dream into reality. And it builds faith that all things are possible with God.

You are programing your mind.
You decide what thoughts belong.
You are in charge! Pay attention.

Chapter 11

THE REFRIGERATOR DOOR TECHNIQUE

One time long ago when our children were small, my husband Jim dreamed of owning his own airplane. He was enjoying an afternoon at the airport looking at the planes when a Cessna 140 caught his eye. He looked it over. They only wanted $22,360.00 for it. At that time, it was a reasonable price, but that was a year's salary, and there was no way he could afford it.

A few days later he went back and took a picture of it and he taped to the refrigerator door. Around the picture he wrote: "I want it! I deserve it! I have it!" Every time he went to the refrigerator he said, "I want it! I deserve it! I have it!" Sometimes he even patted the picture. A few weeks went by. He continued his daily affirmations.

One day, his insurance agent called to see if he needed more insurance. " Hell no! I want an airplane!" was his reply. Where did that come from? Still today it is a mystery. His subconscious spoke for him. He had programed his mind by using this technique.

There was a long pause on the other end. "Well," said his agent, " You know you have three paid up policies, with a cash value." "How much?" was Jims' question."There might be enough, and you would not have to repay it. I'll get back to you," was the response from the Insurance salesman. Jim thought no more about it, dismissed it completely. A few days later, his

agent called."I have good news and bad news."
"I'll take the good news,"Jim said, hardly
remembering their former conversation." All I
can get you is $23,000. No pay back."

Needless to say he bought his Cessna 140 and
had many hours of pleasure flying it. He owned
three other airplanes after that, all in some way
generated by his Refrigerator Door Treasure Map.

When we wanted a tractor to mow the grass on
our dream ranch in Northern California, he
investigated thoroughly and decided on a
Ford 1600. We were busy paying for the
property and improving it. There was no way to
afford another payment.

He put a picture of it on the refrigerator door
with," I want it! I deserve it! I have it!" It was
only $200.00 a month payment, but at that
time, it seemed impossible.

A friend called asking Jim to be an insurance
representative after school for a few hours a
week. The pay was $200.00 a month. That
summer he mowed his own meadow grass
and a few neighbors' grass, as well.

When Jim wanted a new car, we went to town
several times trying to find exactly what he
wanted. Finally, he put a picture of the model
he wanted on the refrigerator door. Nothing
happened. We went to the agencies again. We
found what he wanted , but a different color. By
the time he called to clinch the deal, it was
sold to someone else.

One day a dealer called. He would bring a car to us, no easy matter, as we live two hours away on a mountain road.The car was exactly the same as the picture on the refrigerator door and was the price we were planning to pay.

When Jim wanted a backhoe, there seemed to be some problem. But the problem was mostly that he couldn't make up his mind exactly what he wanted. He put a picture up on the refrigerator door. A few weeks later a dealer lent him the exact model for a week. He tried it. Our dirt was too hard. So the backhoe was returned, and the picture came off the door. He studied and looked the backhoe situation over thoroughly. Finally, a picture of a backhoe appeared again on the refrigerator door. It was barely three weeks until we had a new backhoe for his use. This one is completely satisfactory.

Ido not intend to imply that these items came free or that we purchased them with no way to make the payments. The Universe always provided for our needs. Sometimes the item was free, but most of the time, the opportunity was provided, our goals were achieved. Some items are hard to find in rural areas but the Universe filled our orders exactly.

A dear friend lived even farther out on a ten-mile dirt road. She wanted a telephone as she was going into a business, and a telephone was a vital part. The Telephone Company was promising telephones in her area in 5-8 years. But she needed one now. She put a picture of a telephone on her propane refrigerator door. It was not even a month when she received a

The Soden Home
Still under construction.

Jim's Backhoe

What is Your Dream? Write About It.

notice in the mail. Telephones were being extended down her road. In two months she had her much-needed telephone.

The Universe provides for all our needs. We only have to believe that it does and open our minds to accept our blessings.

Do not be concerned with how it will come about. The how is none of your business. Do not spend any time, or thought on the HOW as this is the Universe's, GOD department. It does not hurt to notice or observe the way it comes about.

I am reminded frequently of this Principle as I do the dishes. The Universe is likened to the water facet turned on full. We can hold our container up to that inflow and receive all that God is giving of every good thing or we can cover our container with a lid and nothing enters. If we filter the inflow (like putting a sieve over the opening) we receive only a small portion of God's blessings. The sieve could represent our resistance, our unbelief. Many of us have stopped believing in God's givingness, resulting in a nation with many people in want. Positive thinking starts us in the right direction but using the power of belief opens the door.

What exactly are you doing when you use the Refrigerator Door technique? We know that our minds need many exposures to an idea in order to unlearn anything. The Refrigerator Door technique gives you as many exposures each day as the times you open or pass by the door. The Universe, God, acts on the pictures contained in your mind. If your mind is focused on a new house or car, the action of the Law of God uses that mental pattern as a basis for blessing you.

I suggest that you use "I want it. I deserve it. I have it. Thank you, God" as a means to build your faith in God's ever-providing nature. Prove the Law, "It is done unto you as you believe." / 1 Matt. 8.13

Chapter 12

LAW OF GIVING AND RECEIVING

No discussion of prosperity is complete without addressing the circle of giving and receiving. When you give, you begin the action of the Universe. The circle is completed when your gift is returned to you multiplied. Knowing this, Universal Principle does not limit your use of it, nor does not knowing. But now that you know, why not use your knowledge to prosper yourself.

The Law of Giving and Receiving is basic to learning how to use God's Principles. If you are not of a giving nature, start a new chapter in your life. Give of your surplus, give of your overflow. Make it a point to give something to someone every day. As you get into the stream of giving and receiving, you will discover that you lack for no good thing.

Life is somewhat like a card game. You get to play the cards you were dealt. By using the Principles you can change the hand you are holding from losing to winning.

Be alert. If an opportunity comes for overtime work, do it thankfully. If a friend needs help, volunteer. Living on the mountain top in consciousness is great, but living in the world is also great and requires greatness from us.

When you give to the Universe, it is a circle. What you give out, you receive back multiplied. "And when Jesus sat in front of the treasury, many rich men were casting in a great deal.

And there came a poor widow woman, and she cast in two coins, which are a few pennies. And Jesus called His disciples and said to them, "Truly I say to you that this poor widow has cast into the treasury more than all the men who are casting; for all of them cast in of their abundance; but she of her poverty cast everything she had, even all of her possessions'."/1

The widow put her complete trust in the Universe and began a circle. What she gave, she received back multiplied. Practice using this Principle in as many ways as you can. Prove it to yourself.

I remember a woman who never let anyone leave her home without something in hand, a flower, a potholder, something she had raised or made. She gave freely of herself to all who passed her way.

The people of this country are of a most generous nature. This was brought to mind again when a young man came to our door on a two-year mission to walk about this country listening to people's ideas about education, ways of restructuring our schools, financing, and emphasizing the importance of education. He found many an outstretched hand that give him food, shelter, and ideas along the way. He remembered the last town he visited, "I hardly got into town that late afternoon with my pack on my back when a man came up to me and asked, "Do you have a place to stay tonight?" Ron said, he did not. "See that blue house over there. You go there and they'll take care of you." /1 Mark 12.41-44

He went there and knocked on the door. A man came to the door. Taking one look at my friend he said,"Supper's on. Come in and sit down." They cared for him very well that night.

When we give without expecting anything in return, we give from the heart; so to speak, we become instruments of God. The blessing comes immediately and automatically. Do you feel especially glad that you can give? This attitude of gratitude that you can share of your bounty with others makes you doubly blessed. Even if it is, in a small way that you feel good when you do it. Give with love and joy.

Is it acceptable for people to be rich? So much has been taught in our culture that to be poor is to be Godly. The Apostle Paul wrote: "Charge those who are rich in this world that they be not proud, nor trust in the uncertainty of riches, but in the living God who gives us all things so abundantly for our comfort. That they do good works, and become rich in good deeds, and be ready to give and willing to share. Laying up in store for them a good foundation against the time to come, that they may lay hold upon the true life."/2 So, it is OK to be rich and to use your riches for yourself and give to others.

What about giving ideas, sharing your visions or giving your wisdom, pearls of great price to others./3 "Do not throw your pearls before swine." Be wise. Listen to your inner voice before you speak and follow its direction even if you have to put your hand over your mouth. Spend /2 I Timothy 6.17-19, /3 Matthew 7.6

your time with those of like mind who are seeking the Truth where you can speak freely.

I have observed that Ross Perot used the Principles of the Universe right in front of our eyes. It was reported he gave millions to the Salvation Army for the flood victims when the Mississippi River overflowed its banks. You may say, "He won't miss it. He's got millions more." That is how he got his millions: by giving, and giving and giving. The Universe returned to him all that he had given plus much more.

I've heard that the poor country of Bangladesh sent burlap bags and tea when they heard of our disaster. They gave of what they had.

This reminds me of a little old jingle John Bunyan gave us:

"There was a man they called him mad.
The more he gave, the more he had."

When we give of ourself, our goods, our time, or our attention, we are giving from an Infinite Source. The more we give, the more there is to give. Trust the Infinite to give you a bountiful return. Don't keep mental books. Just trust that what you need you will have on time and perfectly fulfilling. No lack or limitation to it.

The great Bibles and religious books of the world proclaim: give freely of your goods and you will have more. The ancient Chinese teachings say, "the more we give to others, the more we have." It is the Principle of returning of the self to the

Self. Karma means the fruit of the action, a circle that works automatically to bring to the actor the result of the action, multiplied.

Emerson called it the Law of Compensation.
/4 The Master Jesus is reported to have given generously to the poor and taught to " Give and it shall be given unto you; good measure, pressed down, and shaken together, and running over, shall men give unto your bosom. For with the same measure that ye mete withal it shall be measured to you again."/5 In Jesus' time it was not at all uncommon to give up to 40% of ones income to the Temple and who did so still prospered.

Give to the Source of Your Spiritual Support

We must always give back to the Source equal measure of the gift to us. If your church has given you inspiration, direction, spiritual support or physical support, it is worthy of your regular identifiable dependable tithe. If your Practitioner has been there for you, your part is to return that pledge in monetary means. If the word tithe is uncomfortable to you, use another word, but give nonetheless.

People ask me if giving to the homeless or other good cause is the same. NO! give to those after you have given to your Spiritual Source. Spiritual growth can be obstructed at this one point. If your desire is Spiritual growth, you must leave no stones unturned. Give to your church! /4 Essays;Ralph Waldo Emerson.
/5 Luke 6.38

Receiving

You may say that giving is easy. It's receiving that's hard. Are you suspicious of people who give you things? Perhaps there are some hidden strings or they want something. Some people feel giving gifts is buying friendship. What a lot of negative ideas we have built up to limit our use of the Law of Giving and Receiving.

When in doubt start back at the basic premise of the Law that implies that to give and receive is good, and that blessings untold can be the result when we learn to do so with spontaneity, with joy, with love, and without thought. Putting all else aside, begin by giving of what you have at hand and accepting the gifts that are given to you graciously and with thanksgiving to the person giving and to God the giver of all good and perfect gifts. By stepping up to the higher uses of the law you increase the return many fold.

If you are still hesitant or resist or feel you don't deserve to receive good gifts, work needs to be done on the inner belief to alleviate these limited views.

YOU DESERVE IT! ACCEPT IT! Begin your daily review of your Treasure Map with these words. I DESERVE IT! I ACCEPT IT ! God is giving to me pressed down and shaken together and running over, today.

The Principle of the Open Hand

The Principle of the Open Hand is an important part of the use of the Law of Increase. The Master Jesus stretched forth His hands to heal the sick and give to the poor. Can you imagine Him stretching forth his hands in a fist? Not at all. He stretched forth His open hands and gave to all. Stretch forth your giving hand open and you will receive equal measure. Prosperity doesn't come to closed hands nor does it stay in a tight grasp. A tight grasp always destroys.

God is eternally giving with an open hand. There is no lack in this world. God gives all to create this universe and sustain it. All is being given, but we do not always see or recognize the gifts. When it comes through people, we tend to think it's not a gift from God. Relax and let God provide. We can think of only a few channels through which our good can come. God uses an infinite number to provide for Its Divine Children. Open your eyes and mind to accept the gifts that are given to you. Open your hands and give. You shall receive. I love this Psalm: "Thou openest thy hand and satisfieth the desire of every living thing." /6 This is the Truth for the microcosm (us) and the Macrocosm (God). Learn to use the Law of Increase for your benefit./6 Psalms 146.16

Chapter 13

HOW TO LIVE A PROSPEROUS LIFE

Is it your desire to live a prosperous life? Do you yearn to get out of debt and stay out? You may hope to do this some time and it may become a reality, but hoping, believing and knowing ar. just a line of progressive thinking. The whole world is hoping, and has been hoping for generations. We need to step up from hoping to believing that a prosperous life is ours now. The more you believe it is the Truth, the more evidence accumulates that it is the Truth. When you move into Knowing, you prove your belief over and over again and you KNOW.

It is possible to live comfortably every day of your life with all your needs met. You will discover that this level of living comes as you understand and live the principles. Such things as competition (belief that something can be taken away from you), or lack (belief that there is a limited supply) hoarding or greed, (belief in other Gods), condemning others' choice of paths (only one way, my way); beliefs of this nature must be overcome. As you become purer in heart, you will discover that all your needs are met before you ask. In the rarefied air of living in God's Grace you will discover that one of the blessings is an abundance of every good thing coming to you unbidden. You have the opportunity to focus this good into areas of your choice.

Choose the Highest and the Best First

A group of young students asked their learned rabbi whether one should, in eating a bunch of grapes, eat the best grapes first or last. His answer, "Always eat the best first and you'll always be eating the best." So choose the best, your greatest desire, and you will discover that it isn't any harder than settling for a lesser choice.

Goal Setting and Goal Reaching

Time to set some goals in your life? Goals can be for things and/or for higher levels of consciousness. You will discover that when you set a goal from your logical left brain, some part must be played by your feeling, sensing right brain. We recommend choosing goals that come from both hemispheres and will develop more faith in God's goodness.

Steps to Obtain Your Dream

FIRST: You have to know exactly what you want. If you don't know what you want, you will go on accepting what the world has to offer and nothing more, just wandering through life believing whatever will be,will be (like the French song).

SECOND: Write it down. Make a list. Don't forget any part or leave it to chance. Make a plan to complete in six months. Then extend yourself. Write where you desire to be on your plan in one year, and then in five years. Project what you want to be happening in ten years.

THIRD: Start a diary. Record your plan on the front pages. Daily make entries of the actions you have taken that day to implement your plan and the result. Why is this method effective? When you make up your mind, make a list or a plan that is focusing creative energies to bring these blessings about. List-making clears the mind and your life situation. Be sure your list contains that which you really desire and is a blessing to everyone concerned. Know that it will come about in a gentle loving manner, as a whisper in the ear.

Leave it open at the top. <u>This desire or something better.</u> Always leave room   for

SOMETHING BETTER!

In order to create a vacuum, you need to review the things that you wish to eliminate from your life: feelings of envy, forgiveness of yourself and others, overcoming attitudes of poverty. Poverty attitudes are automatic thoughts that say: "I can't afford it.' or "I'm not into money." You've heard the comment, "They don't make them like they used to". Pay attention to those negative thoughts and feelings like, "I don't deserve it." Eliminate negative ideas. Stop those negative ideas in their tracks.

It is a physical law that a vacuum must be filled. Fill it with beauty, love, peace of mind, and prosperity. Millions of people have proved this Law and reprogrammed their lives. You can do it too!

BE THANKFUL for the blessing you have. Thank God daily for life and for every other blessing you have, and the blessings you desire. Don't differentiate between them. Just give thanks.

Realize Your Million

Have you got your million dollars yet? Why not? Winning a million dollars is entirely possible these days. Not yet? Why not? Because you have not been able to visualize yourself as having a million dollars. Maybe you began to believe that you could have it in your thought, enjoyed the excitement of getting it. Then began to wonder if it would change your life. Then you wondered if you would like that change, and before you knew it, you talked yourself out of it completely.

Let's discuss how you get ideas that will make you a million. To begin, the Universe is filled with ideas, creative, never used before, marvelous ideas. And they are available to anyone who is clear minded enough to reach out for them. These ideas are everywhere equally available, so you don't have to go anywhere to receive them. They are right where you are now.

The secret is being clear minded enough to reach inside yourself, listen, accept and act on the ideas that come through you. Set your list of requirements clearly; for example: I desire to find a way to make a better mouse trap. Open your mind to receive ideas and be willing to try them out. How many people have wished they had invested in new ideas when they become popular. There are still plenty of ideas available for your development.

89

If your desire is to retire early with enough income to support yourself and your family in the manner you are accustomed, in the place you desire to live, it is possible. Complete the picture: keeping yourself active, interested in life, physically healthy and able to pursue your life long interests, being independent and free enough to travel. This life can be your life, now!

Think of your desires as the input to a giant computer which you program confidently, then await the action to come about in reality. Many answers to your request are possible. There are many just right for you, all of which will perfectly answer your need. So start by clearly setting in your mind exactly what you desire your life to be like. This is the pattern or the mold or the input. It's OK to desire a million dollars.

Pay close attention to the the first idea that comes. Symbolically that is the answer. The first idea or solution has the most power and, though it may seem impossible, that is the greatest and best idea.

It is important that through this entire process you keep your own counsel. You are not asking for the ideas of friends or loved ones. You are asking the Universal Mind and the answer will come entirely from the pool of Universal ideas perfectly suited to your needs and desires.

What do you do when you know what the right way is? You begin to mentally start in that direction. Look for ways to implement that idea. When ideas present themselves, confidently act on them knowing that you are correctly led. When the first idea comes, keep quiet about it as you begin implementing it. And do not let other people prematurely talk you out of your good idea.

There is an old story told about Alexander Graham Bell. After inventing the telephone and placing his company on the stock market, he realized that the telephone stock was going to be a good investment. So he went to the bank, drew out his life savings of $30,000. and started down to the stock market to invest in telephone stock. On the way he met a friend and made the mistake of sharing his idea with him. The friend only laughed at Mr. Bell, and then talked him into redepositing his $30,000 in the bank. Mr. Bell later mourned, " Thanks to my friend, I just missed becoming a millionaire."

If you have let someone talk you out of your good, it can be restored. Just begin again.

The Universe is an endless supply of divine ideas just waiting for you. So begin again.

1. Ask for a great idea that will benefit yourself and the world.
2. Ask how to implement it. Practice seeing the first step.
3. Let go of inharmonious, limited thinking.
4. Be sure to act in greatest integrity. Use the idea as directed.
5. If you promise anything as a result of this process, fulfill your promise.
6. Never forget where this gift came from. THANK GOD!

If you are feeling overwhelmed by the immensity of the task before you, don't be. You do not have to move the world, just change your thought.
How do you eat an apple pie? One bite at a time.

Begin your plan that will change your life and also change the world.

Begin today! You can do it. Pay attention!

BIBLIOGRAPHY

Bartholomew, Stella: *The Power of Love in Graphic Prayer*, Fish Rock Publishing Co. 1977
Emerson, Ralph Waldo: *Essays*, A.L. Burt Company Publishers. New York, N.Y. Vol.I
Lamsa, George M. *The Holy Bible*, A.J. Holman Co. Philadelphia, 1957
Soden, Alyce Bartholomew: *Parenting the Enlightened Child*, Fish Rock Publishing Co 1997

RECOMMENDED READING

Amazing Secrets of Psychic Healing by Benjamin O. Bib,, Parker Publishing Co. West Nyack, N.Y. (out of print) using a visual method is described in greater detail.

The Power of Love in Graphic Prayer by Stella Bartholomew, Fish Rock Publishers, 33801 So. Hwy. I Gualala. (707) 884-3631

Parenting the Enlightened Child by Alyce Bartholomew Soden, 1997 Fish Rock Publishers, 33801 So. Hwy.I Gualala, CA 95445 (707) 884-3631 FAX 884-3630

Depression Be Gone by Alyce Bartholomew Soden, 1996 Fish Rock Publications(As above)

Jish Rock Publications
33801 So. Hwy. I, Gualala, CA 95445
(707) 884-3631 FAX (707) 884-3630
E-MAIL soden@mcn.org